Midweek Meditations

Debra J. K. Bronkema

Midweek Meditations
ISBN: Softcover 978-1-951472-80-1
Copyright © 2020 by Debra Bronkema

All rights reserved. No part of this book may be reproduced or transmitted in any form or by any means, electronic or mechanical, including photocopying, recording, or by any information storage and retrieval system, without permission in writing from the publisher.

Parson's Porch Books is an imprint of Parson's Porch & Company (PP&C) in Cleveland, Tennessee. PP&C is an innovative organization which raises money by publishing books of noted authors, representing all genres. Its face and voice is **David Russell Tullock** (dtullock@parsonsporch.com).

Parson's Porch & Company *turns books into bread* by sharing its profits with the poor.

www.parsonsporch.com

Midweek Meditations

Contents

Dedication 9
Acknowledgements 11
(1) What Time is it? 13
    Ecclesiastes 3:1-8
(2) God Speaks 15
    Matthew 2:1-12
(3) All Means All 17
    Acts 10:34-35,43
(4) Come and See 19
    John 1:35-42
(5) Listening for God 21
    Romans 12:1-2
(6) Justice, Kindness, and Humility 23
    Micah 6:8
(7) Challenge and Comfort 25
    Isaiah 58:6-7,10-11
(8) Dwelling on the Mountaintop 27
    Matthew 17:1-4
(9) A Clean Heart 29
    Psalm 51:1-2, 6-12
(10) Reflections on Lent 31
    Matthew 4:1-11
(11) Water and Faith 33
    John 4:7-10
(12) The Lord is My Shepherd 35
    Psalm 23
(13) The Great Invitation 37
    Matthew 11:28-30
(14) Holy Week is Coming! 39
    Psalm 118.1
(15) On the Way 41
    Matthew 26:6-13
(16) Christ is Risen! 43
    John 20:11-18

(17) Celebrating God's Gift of Creation 45
    Genesis 1:1-3, 28-31
(18) A New Thing 47
    Isaiah 43:18-19
(19) What is Love? 49
    1 John 4:7-12
(20) Filling Up 51
    Psalm 42:1-2,4-5
(21) Renewed Strength 53
    Isaiah 40:28-31
(22) Beyond Boundaries 55
    Numbers 11:24-30
(23) Built Together 57
    Ephesians 2:17-22
(24) Lay Your Worries Down 59
    Matthew 6:25,33-34
(25) Welcoming 61
    Matthew 10:40-42
(26) Discernment 63
    Jeremiah 28:5-9
(27) Meditating on our Faith 65
    Psalm 145:1-5
(28) God's Word Breaking In 67
    Isaiah 55:10-12
(29) An Undivided Heart 69
    Psalm 86:11-13
(30) Wisdom 71
    1 Kings 3:5-12
(31) On The Heart 73
    Jeremiah 31:31-34
(32) Sheer Silence 75
    1 Kings 19:9-12
(33) Transformation 77
    Romans 12:1-2
(34) Moving Day 79
    1 Corinthians 13:4-7, 12-13

(35) Companions on the Journey 81
    Jeremiah 15:16
(36) Proverbs for Today 83
    Proverbs 4:20-23
(37) Seventy-seven times 85
    Matthew 18:21-22
(38) Jonah, the Whale and Us 87
    Jonah 1:1-4, 13-17, 2:10
(39) Pathways 89
    Psalm 25:4-5
(40) Unity 91
    Psalm 133
(41) Think on These Things 93
    Philippians 4:8-9
(42) Called By Name 95
    Isaiah 45:1-3
(43) What is in Our Hearts? 97
    Deuteronomy 6:4-9
(44) When I Am Afraid 99
    Psalm 34:4-8
(45) Today! 101
    Psalm 70:1,4-5
(46) Treasures 103
    Matthew 6:19-21
(47) Giving Thanks 105
    Ephesians 1:15-19
(48) Happy Thanksgiving Eve! 107
    Galatians 5:22-23
(49) Overcoming Fear 109
    Matthew 24:36-44
(50) Accepting the Invitation to Repentance 111
    Matthew 3:1-6
(51) The Wolf and the Lamb 113
    Isaiah 11:1-2, 6-7
(52) Merry Christmas! 115
    John 1:1-4, 14

Dedication

Midweek Meditations is dedicated to

My husband John

My children Cali, Dylan, Logan and Caleb

My parents Ronald and Marilyn Kevern

with much gratitude for their love and support.

Acknowledgements

I want to thank the churches and ministries that have nurtured me on my faith journey as a child, pastor and writer over the years. Thank you to St. Paul's United Methodist Church, in Rochester Michigan, Princeton United Methodist Church, in Princeton, New Jersey, Basking Ridge Presbyterian Church, in Basking Ridge, New Jersey, Presbyterian Church of the Master, in Omaha, Nebraska, First Presbyterian Church of Sussex, in Sussex, New Jersey, Cedarkirk Presbyterian Camp and Conference Center, in Lithia, Florida, First Presbyterian Church of Brandon, in Brandon, Florida and Pleasantville Presbyterian Church, in Pleasantville, New York, and connect.faith, a new worshiping community of the PCUSA. I have learned so much from, and been so blessed to be part of, each of these communities.

Midweek Meditations began as a weekly email series designed for Pleasantville Presbyterian Church, where I've served as Pastor for over thirteen years. I'm grateful for the support and encouragement to grow in ministry that they've always given me.

Most of all, I'm thankful to my family for all their help and love along the way.

(1) What Time is it?

Ecclesiastes 3:1-8

For everything there is a season, and a time for every matter under heaven:

a time to be born, and a time to die;

a time to plant, and a time to pluck up what is planted;

a time to kill, and a time to heal; a time to break down, and a time to build up; a time to weep, and a time to laugh; a time to mourn, and a time to dance.

a time to throw away stones, and a time to gather stones together; a time to embrace, and a time to refrain from embracing.

a time to seek, and a time to lose; a time to keep, and a time to throw away; a time to tear, and a time to sew; a time to keep silence, and a time to speak; a time to love, and a time to hate; a time for war, and a time for peace.

Devotion:

What time is it? What time is it in each of our lives? In our life together as children of God? Are we open to healing, planting, mourning, dancing? What time is it?

Living an intentional life of faith means paying attention to how we spend the gift of each day. It means noticing time and living in the present moment, and letting the present moment live in us.

As the new year begins may we ask ourselves questions about how we feel called to use this amazing gift of time we've been given.

Prayer:

Dear God, help us to be open to the gifts that you have given us, and will continue to give us in this new year. Help us to say yes to you - and embrace the time we are in as an opportunity to grow in faith in you. Amen

Reflection Questions:

1. Really, what time is it for you?

2. What time is it for the people in your life?

3. What is one thing you can do to live in God's time today?

(2) God Speaks

Matthew 2:1-12

In the time of King Herod, after Jesus was born in Bethlehem of Judea, wise men from the East came to Jerusalem, asking, "Where is the child who has been born king of the Jews? For we observed his star at its rising and have come to pay him homage." When King Herod heard this, he was frightened, and all Jerusalem with him; and calling together all the chief priests and scribes of the people, he inquired of them where the Messiah was to be born. They told him, "In Bethlehem of Judea; for so it has been written by the prophet:

'And you, Bethlehem, in the land of Judah, are by no means least among the rulers of Judah; for from you shall come a ruler who is to shepherd my people Israel.'"

Then Herod secretly called for the wise men and learned from them the exact time when the star had appeared. Then he sent them to Bethlehem, saying, "Go and search diligently for the child; and when you have found him, bring me word so that I may also go and pay him homage." When they had heard the king, they set out; and there, ahead of them, went the star that they had seen at its rising, until it stopped over the place where the child was. When they saw that the star had stopped, they were overwhelmed with joy. On entering the house, they saw the child with Mary his mother; and they knelt down and paid him homage. Then, opening their treasure chests, they offered him gifts of gold, frankincense, and myrrh. And having been warned in a dream not to return to Herod, they left for their own country by another road.

Devotion:

This is familiar Scripture – the kind it helps to read slowly out loud, so that we can hear it in a new way.

When I tried that this time – I heard the cunning words of Herod. He plays on the naivete of the wise men and tries to fool them into being part of his Kingly plan to eliminate all who might threaten his power.

So, what does God do? God gives them a dream and sends them back by a different way. God gives them a dream in order to accomplish God's mission. These wise men, they are people of stars and dreams. God knows us and God speaks in the language we need to hear.

Prayer:

Dear God – Help me to be open to how you are speaking to me today. Help me to listen for you and trust that you are in this with us. In Jesus Name – Amen

Reflection Questions:

1) What language do you think God would speak to get your attention?

2) Try reading this or another familiar scripture out loud. What do you hear?

3) How can you open up more ways for God to break into your day-to-day life?

(3) All Means All
Acts 10:34-35,43

> *Then Peter began to speak to them: "I truly understand that God shows no partiality, but in every nation anyone who fears him and does what is right is acceptable to him.*
>
> *All the prophets testify about him that everyone who believes in him receives forgiveness of sins through his name."*

Devotion:

Right here, right now – it really feels like we need to be reminded to value all people. To pay attention to the news and care about what happens, not just here, but everywhere. To consider what we can do to let people know that we are all in this together – and that God's grace and forgiveness is for everybody.

Forgiveness is one of the biggest challenges we face as humans. Forgiving others, forgiving ourselves, asking for forgiveness, praying for forgiveness - in all of these places our humanity struggles. We all need to hear about how God opens up forgiveness and asks us to look at the power of grace.

I believe the power of the Holy Spirit is in us – and walks with us in times of joy and in times of struggle. Right now – the world needs us to bring the love and forgiveness and grace of Christ with us to every interaction we have – and be instruments of peace.

Prayer:

Dear God, May I know today that your love knows no boundaries – and if I want to follow you – I need to do my best to reflect that love to my corner of the world. Amen

Reflection Questions:

1) When has God challenged your perspective on who is included in the grace of God?

2) How is God challenging you to show no partiality today?

3) How can you live out your faith story – without using words?

(4) Come and See
John 1:35-42

> *The next day John again was standing with two of his disciples, and as he watched Jesus walk by, he exclaimed, "Look, here is the Lamb of God!" The two disciples heard him say this, and they followed Jesus. When Jesus turned and saw them following, he said to them, "What are you looking for?" They said to him, "Rabbi" (which translated means Teacher), "where are you staying?" He said to them, "Come and see." They came and saw where he was staying, and they remained with him that day. It was about four o'clock in the afternoon. One of the two who heard John speak and followed him was Andrew, Simon Peter's brother. He first found his brother Simon and said to him, "We have found the Messiah" (which is translated Anointed). He brought Simon to Jesus, who looked at him and said, "You are Simon son of John. You are to be called Cephas" (which is translated Peter).*

Devotion:

This passage in which the Disciples and Jesus begin their journey together makes me wonder what it would be like to be in that scene. Where would we be standing? How would we answer Jesus' question about what we are looking for? What would he rename us?

What happens if we think about Jesus walking down Main Street? What do we see Jesus doing and saying, if he was meeting us on the road today? Would we be open to hearing what he had to say – or would we be rushing on our own way – missing the moment at hand?

Today - let's read the passage and picture ourselves along the way. Would we choose to "Come and See," if Jesus invited us to join him on the way?

Prayer:

Dear God - Please help me "Come and See" the Jesus who invites us on a journey of discipleship with him. In Jesus Name, Amen

Reflection Questions:

1) Today: what are you searching for?

2) If you imagine yourself in this scene - where are you standing? Who are you standing beside?

3) If Jesus invited you to follow him to an unknown destination - what would you say?

(5) Listening for God
Romans 12:1-2

> *I appeal to you therefore, brothers and sisters, by the mercies of God, to present your bodies as a living sacrifice, holy and acceptable to God, which is your spiritual worship. Do not be conformed to this world, but be transformed by the renewing of your minds, so that you may discern what is the will of God— what is good and acceptable and perfect*

Devotion:

I am sitting on a porch in the middle of winter, because I am in Florida as I write this. The retreat center, Cedarkirk Presbyterian Camp and Conference Center has a wonderful wide porch full of rocking chairs that look out onto a slice of nature, and a weathered wooden cross that seems as though it is ten feet tall. A man at the other end of the porch says as he rocks, "Lots of life decisions made on this porch." I am sure it's true. At a place apart we do listen better for God's words in response to our need.

No matter where we are - in the warmth of Florida, in the winter in New York, in our own living room - we can make spaces, moments to open our hearts and souls and hear what God has to say. We can make room for the love of God to help us discern the life decisions that we make, day by day by day.

Prayer:

Dear God, please help me to listen to you today, tomorrow and all the days of my life. Help me to make space and time for you. In Jesus Name, Amen

Reflection Questions:

1) What decisions are you trying to make today?

2) How can you make space to listen to God?

3) Try sitting quietly and writing whatever comes to you in the moment. It's okay if it's a grocery list - just open yourself to listen.

(6) Justice, Kindness, and Humility
Micah 6:8

> *He has told you, O mortal, what is good; and what does the Lord require of you but to do justice, and to love kindness, and to walk humbly with your God?*

Devotion:

It's one of the verses in the Bible that we might feel like we've heard before. It's helpful on those days when we want an answer – what do you want from me Lord? Oh, that's right - Micah 6:8.

On the other hand – there's nothing simple about this verse. In fact, I think it deserves some time in contemplation. How do these words sound in the middle of your life right now? Where do you find them challenging? Where do you see them as affirming of your way of life? How might they help you discern something you're struggling with – or show you a path that you haven't noticed?

Prayer:

Dear God, I am thankful for this verse. I am thankful that you help us try to understand what it looks like to follow you. I am thankful – even when I realize just how far I have to go. In Jesus Name, Amen

Reflection Questions:

1) Which word is easiest for you to consider – justice, kindness, or humility?

2) Which word is hardest?

3) How do you think you can take a step toward what the Lord wants of you today?

(7) Challenge and Comfort
Isaiah 58:6-7,10-11

> *Is not this the fast that I choose: to loose the bonds of injustice, to undo the thongs of the yoke, to let the oppressed go free, and to break every yoke?*
>
> *Is it not to share your bread with the hungry, and bring the homeless poor into your house; when you see the naked, to cover them, and not to hide yourself from your own kin? If you offer your food to the hungry and satisfy the needs of the afflicted, then your light shall rise in the darkness and your gloom be like the noonday. The LORD will guide you continually, and satisfy your needs in parched places, and make your bones strong; and you shall be like a watered garden, like a spring of water, whose waters never fail.*

Devotion:

I think about this scripture reading a lot. It's one of those that continually both challenges and comforts me. It says that we are all in this together. That how we treat each other matters to God. That our souls will find more peace when we choose to share what we have with people who need it. It says that when we are paying attention, we can hear God calling us again and again to be present to the people we meet on our journey. Whether they are hungry of body or soul – there are people needing us to show up for them, and that showing up will set us free from the things that are binding us as well.

Look – we all know that life around us is getting self-centered. So – let's try living today with Isaiah 58 eyes. I wonder what might happen if we do!

Prayer:

Dear God, Thank you for not letting us get comfortable with a world view that says, "What's in it for me?" Help us stand up and be present to your people in need, wherever we find them. Amen

Reflection Questions:

1) Do you remember a time when helping someone else filled your soul too?

2) What can you do today to live with an Isaiah 58 perspective?

3) Do you think self-centeredness is a problem in our society – or is it more of an individual issue?

(8) Dwelling on the Mountaintop
Matthew 17:1-4

> *Six days later, Jesus took with him Peter and James and his brother John and led them up a high mountain, by themselves. And he was transfigured before them, and his face shone like the sun, and his clothes became dazzling white. Suddenly there appeared to them Moses and Elijah, talking with him. Then Peter said to Jesus, "Lord, it is good for us to be here; if you wish, I will make three dwellings here, one for you, one for Moses, and one for Elijah."*

Devotion:

I've always loved how Peter sees the amazing glory of the moment in front of him and wants to build dwelling places for Jesus and Moses and Elijah – so that they can all live there forever.

Have you ever had a spiritual moment that you wanted to build a house around – and live there forever? A time when you felt close to God, a place where you sensed that there was a connection between God and humanity that you didn't ever want to move away from?

These mountaintop moments help sustain us on the valley days of our journey. For many people – though we find the mountaintop moments in all kinds of places – it is in worship that we find that connecting point again – amplified in our lives in a way that reminds us who and whose we are. I hope as the seasons of Lent and springtime approach, we can open ourselves up to however God is trying to get our attention.

Prayer:

Dear God – "Open my eyes that I may see visions of truth thou hast for me." May the words of the hymn be the words of my prayer this week. In Jesus Name – Amen

Reflection Questions:

1) Consider if you've ever had something you'd call a mountaintop moment on your faith journey.

2) Write or draw the image this moment recalls.

3) Is there a hymn or a song that gives you the feeling of connecting closely with God?

(9) A Clean Heart
Psalm 51:1-2, 6-12

Have mercy on me, O God, according to your steadfast love; according to your abundant mercy blot out my transgressions.

Wash me thoroughly from my iniquity, and cleanse me from my sin.

You desire truth in the inward being therefore teach me wisdom in my secret heart. Purge me with hyssop, and I shall be clean; wash me, and I shall be whiter than snow.

Let me hear joy and gladness; let the bones that you have crushed rejoice.

Hide your face from my sins and blot out all my iniquities. Create in me a clean heart, O God, and put a new and right spirit within me. Do not cast me away from your presence, and do not take your holy spirit from me. Restore to me the joy of your salvation and sustain in me a willing spirit.

Devotion:

Create in me a clean heart – there is something visually healing to me in those words.

I imagine God helping me look inside to find the places where sin is making me feel broken. I imagine God helping me lay aside my denial, my guilt, all the things that get in the way of living the life of faith I want to live.

This scripture is a perfect one to help us find the genuine part of ourselves and let the breath of the Spirit breathe through us. To be honest with ourselves, to hear what it is God wants us to hear about the state of our hearts today – this is how we move into joy.

Prayer:

O God - Create in me a clean heart. Please God – help me see the things I don't want to see. Help me move this Lent toward the intentional life of discipleship that I want to live in you. Amen

Reflection Questions:

1) What helps you open yourself to reflect on the state of your heart?

2) What do you want to add to your life this Lent that will help you focus on God?

3) Imagine God helping you clean the sin out of your life. What do you see?

(10) Reflections on Lent
Matthew 4:1-11

Then Jesus was led up by the Spirit into the wilderness to be tempted by the devil. He fasted forty days and forty nights, and afterwards he was famished. The tempter came and said to him, "If you are the Son of God, command these stones to become loaves of bread." But he answered, "It is written, 'One does not live by bread alone, but by every word that comes from the mouth of God.'"

Then the devil took him to the holy city and placed him on the pinnacle of the temple, saying to him, "If you are the Son of God, throw yourself down; for it is written,

'He will command his angels concerning you,' and 'On their hands they will bear you up, so that you will not dash your foot against a stone.'"

Jesus said to him, "Again it is written, 'Do not put the Lord your God to the test.'" Again, the devil took him to a very high mountain and showed him all the kingdoms of the world and their splendor; and he said to him, "All these I will give you, if you will fall down and worship me." Jesus said to him, "Away with you, Satan! for it is written,

'Worship the Lord your God and serve only him.'"

Then the devil left him, and suddenly angels came and waited on him.

Devotion:

I've been thinking about what Lent has meant to me over the years. And this passage – with its 40 days in the wilderness and the fasting – those images provide my earliest memories of how I understood Lent. A time to remember Jesus – a time to not eat something – those were the early part of my Lenten story. Then the rest of the passage came to my attention – and the ideas about putting aside temptations that stop us from getting our priorities straight became a part of the story of what Lent means to me.

Finally, the moment came when I realized that none of this was something I could do on my own. So, I made the commitment to add something to my life each Lent that would help keep my focus where I wanted it to be. Some years – it's a devotional, or a new Bible reading practice. Some years – it's an action that marks the commitment I want to make to God. In any case, what I think now is that Lent is a time to take the time to ask ourselves who and whose we are – and let God help us discover the places where our lives don't align with our answers.

Prayer:

Dear God, please help us to listen to your call to us and find our way to turn from the things that separate us from you. Help us to find our way home to you. Amen

Reflection Questions:

1) Do you think you need to subtract or add something to your life to help you connect with God?

2) What are three temptations you've dealt with in the last month?

3) How can you choose God today?

(11) Water and Faith

John 4:7-10

> *A Samaritan woman came to draw water, and Jesus said to her, "Give me a drink." (His disciples had gone to the city to buy food.) The Samaritan woman said to him, "How is it that you, a Jew, ask a drink of me, a woman of Samaria?" (Jews do not share things in common with Samaritans.) Jesus answered her, "If you knew the gift of God, and who it is that is saying to you, 'Give me a drink,' you would have asked him, and he would have given you living water."*

Devotion:

Water is such a strong image in the journey of faith. Whether water at a well, flowing water in a river, or water that comes to us in baptism, in water we see the promise of the ever-flowing fountain of God's love for us.

I know these days we are living in a time of fear – when one of the best defenses against disease we keep hearing about is washing our hands. Could we use this renewed emphasis as a time to pay attention to the flowing of water – to the ways it comes to us and reminds us of the chance we have to say yes to letting the love of God flow through us?

May God's blessings come to you in all times, and may you know that the love of God is always ready to help you find your way.

Prayer:

Dear God, May I be open to the lessons you teach me along the way – opening my heart to let your love flow through. Amen

Reflection Questions:

1) What role has water played in your life?

2) What does it mean to you that Jesus comes to you in your thirst?

3) How can we look at the present moment as a chance to re-orient ourselves toward God?

(12) The Lord is My Shepherd
Psalm 23

The LORD is my shepherd; I shall not want. He makes me lie down in green pastures; he leads me beside still waters; he restores my soul. He leads me in right paths for his name's sake.

Even though I walk through the darkest valley,

I fear no evil; for you are with me; your rod and your staff— they comfort me.

You prepare a table before me in the presence of my enemies; you anoint my head with oil; my cup overflows.

Surely goodness and mercy shall follow me all the days of my life,

and I shall dwell in the house of the LORD my whole life long.

Devotion:

The Lord is my shepherd. I've been closing my eyes and trying to meditate on these words. To breathe them in and out. The Lord is my shepherd. To picture myself lying in green pastures, walking on the paths near the still waters where my soul can be restored.

We are slowing down - not because we wanted to - but we are slowing down. No sporting events, no movies, we are slowing down. Some of us are afraid. Some of us are more afraid of the slowing down than the virus that has caused it. But that's just because we haven't read enough or learned enough to know the why's. We'll have time for that now - we are slowing down.

The Lord is my shepherd. Please O Lord - meet me near those still waters and show me how to slow down and dwell with you.

Prayer:

Dear God - help us find our souls rest in you. In these troubling times, help us know that you do not, will not, leave us alone. In Jesus Name, Amen

Reflection Questions:

1) What part of slowing down do you look forward to?

2) What part of slowing down is really hard for you?

3) Try closing your eyes and breathing in and out the words - The Lord is my Shepherd. Repeat it until you feel your breathing slow down.

(13) The Great Invitation
Matthew 11:28-30

> *"Come to me, all you that are weary and are carrying heavy burdens, and I will give you rest. Take my yoke upon you and learn from me; for I am gentle and humble in heart, and you will find rest for your souls. For my yoke is easy, and my burden is light."*

Devotion:

The Great Invitation – that's what one writer calls this passage. The invitation to carry our heavy burdens to the Lord – who will lighten the load. You remember that the image of the yoke is one of a mantle being put on two oxen's shoulders – so that they hold the weight together. This is the image that goes with this passage – that we will be yoked to Christ Jesus. That our burdens will be lifted not alone, but with him. And by coming to him, we will share with him– but the yoke will fit – and the load will feel not like a burden but light. And we will find rest for our souls.

We may feel alone – but the truth is we are all in this together. We may be alone in our house – but we do that for the good of each other. And that means we are not alone. Christ carries this burden with us – just as Christ walks with us in all of life – and even unto death. Coming to him now can ease the burden we feel. What do you need to bring, specifically, to God today?

Whatever our burdens, whatever our worries – may we accept the invitation to bring them to Jesus. To ask for his strength, his peace, his love to go with us every step of this journey.

Prayer:

Dear God, we come to you today, at your invitation and say yes to the comfort, and the peace, and the help you want to provide. We come to you to see, again or for the first time, that you are in this with us. May we be filled with the love and grace you provide – holding the yoke you offer lightly on our shoulders. In Jesus Name, Amen

Reflection Questions:

1) What do these words of invitation mean to you right now?

2) What part of the invitation do you need to answer with a yes?

3) Picture yourself with Jesus beside you – what do you want to tell him today?

(14) Holy Week is Coming!
Psalm 118:1

O give thanks to the LORD, for he is good; his steadfast love endures forever!

Devotion:

Did you know that Sunday will be the beginning of Holy Week? It's okay if you didn't. Some of us are even having trouble recognizing what day today is – let alone what Wednesday of which month.

The thing is – this Psalm which is part of the scripture readings we usually read on Palm Sunday – its message is good every day of the week. We give thanks to God, not because we particularly like what we see happening in the world around us. Our gratitude might not be about what's happening now at all. On any given day in our world there are people dealing with illness, job loss, pressure and strain. We can find ways to be grateful in all times, but some of us are having a very hard time right now.

And yet – still we can give thanks to God. Not because everything is going well – but because God's love is with us in it, however it's going. Steadfast love that endures forever. There is no better promise than that.

Right here, right now – may we find it in us to be grateful for something – something we see in front of us, even the smallest thing. And then let us give thanks for the something that is the love of God, under the surface of all of our lives – steadfast - enduring forever.

Prayer:

Dear God, we are trying to pay attention, and notice you – and know we are not alone in this. Help us on that journey. Thank you Lord, for your steadfast love. In Jesus Name, Amen

Reflection Questions:

1) What song helps you remember that God's love is steadfast?

2) Can you remember a time that you really experienced the forgiveness and grace of God, even though you didn't think you deserved it?

3) What's one place in nature that reminds you of the steadfast nature of God's love?

(15) On the Way
Matthew 26:6-13

> *Now while Jesus was at Bethany in the house of Simon the leper, a woman came to him with an alabaster jar of very costly ointment, and she poured it on his head as he sat at the table. But when the disciples saw it, they were angry and said, "Why this waste? For this ointment could have been sold for a large sum, and the money given to the poor." But Jesus, aware of this, said to them, "Why do you trouble the woman? She has performed a good service for me. For you always have the poor with you, but you will not always have me. By pouring this ointment on my body she has prepared me for burial. Truly I tell you, wherever this good news is proclaimed in the whole world, what she has done will be told in remembrance of her."*

Devotion:

The scene we look in on today takes place after Palm Sunday, on the way to the Cross. The disciples are gathered, and the woman comes to the table and pours the costly ointment on the head of Jesus. The woman seems to be understanding something that the others are not ready to see – that Jesus will not be with them always. That this is the time to bless him, to give thanks for him. To prepare him for what is to come.

The disciples are missing the moment. They are worried and objecting on behalf of important things – caring for the poor matters, and unfortunately this verse is sometimes taken out of context to make us think Jesus was saying it's not important. What Jesus was saying – and still says to us – is that there are times when we don't let ourselves see what we need to see. Times when we are distracted, and miss the moment we are in. Even when the distraction seems to be for a good cause – it's important for us to pay attention to God's time, and God's timing.

What time are we in? What moment might we be missing - as we distract ourselves with many important things?

Prayer:

Dear God, may we find our way to this moment. May we open our eyes and let ourselves quiet to hear how we can be thankful for the love and sacrifice of Christ Jesus for us. Amen

Reflection Questions:

1) Have you ever felt like you were too distracted to notice what was really happening in an important moment?

2) What would it look like for you to pay attention to the sacrifice of Jesus this Holy Week?

3) How can gratitude help us not to miss important moments? What three things are you grateful for right now?

(16) Christ is Risen!
John 20:11-18

> *But Mary stood weeping outside the tomb. As she wept, she bent over to look into the tomb; and she saw two angels in white, sitting where the body of Jesus had been lying, one at the head and the other at the feet. They said to her, "Woman, why are you weeping?" She said to them, "They have taken away my Lord, and I do not know where they have laid him." When she had said this, she turned around and saw Jesus standing there, but she did not know that it was Jesus. Jesus said to her, "Woman, why are you weeping? Whom are you looking for?" Supposing him to be the gardener, she said to him, "Sir, if you have carried him away, tell me where you have laid him, and I will take him away." Jesus said to her, "Mary!" She turned and said to him in Hebrew, "Rabbouni!" (which means Teacher). Jesus said to her, "Do not hold on to me, because I have not yet ascended to the Father. But go to my brothers and say to them, 'I am ascending to my Father and your Father, to my God and your God.'" Mary Magdalene went and announced to the disciples, "I have seen the Lord"; and she told them that he had said these things to her.*

Devotion:

Go and tell. Tell the others that they don't have to weep anymore at my tomb. Tell them that this day is the first day of a whole new life, and a whole new world. Tell them that what is past is completed, and now – now is the new day!

Mary went and announced. I love that the Bible uses the word announced. She didn't just say it – she proclaimed it. She announced that she had seen the Lord. She announced that the Lord had talked to her. And in her announcement, the people began to get the idea that what looked like the end was actually the beginning.

May we know in our soul the good news that Mary announced.

May we know that Jesus Christ is Risen Today – He is Risen Indeed!

Prayer:

Dear God, May the new day Mary announces become the new day I see every morning, another day to spend with you and celebrate the resurrection! Amen

Reflection Questions:

1) Jesus Christ is Risen Today! What does that mean to you in this moment right now?

2) Have you ever tried to share your faith with someone? What did you say, or do?

3) What does it mean to you to know that what looks like the end might just be the beginning?

(17) Celebrating God's Gift of Creation
Genesis 1:1-3, 28-31

In the beginning when God created the heavens and the earth, the earth was a formless void and darkness covered the face of the deep, while a wind from God swept over the face of the waters. Then God said, "Let there be light"; and there was light.

God blessed them (humanity), and God said to them, "Be fruitful and multiply, and fill the earth and subdue it; and have dominion over the fish of the sea and over the birds of the air and over every living thing that moves upon the earth." God said, "See, I have given you every plant yielding seed that is upon the face of all the earth, and every tree with seed in its fruit; you shall have them for food. And to every beast of the earth, and to every bird of the air, and to everything that creeps on the earth, everything that has the breath of life, I have given every green plant for food." And it was so. God saw everything that he had made, and indeed, it was very good. And there was evening and there was morning, the sixth day.

Devotion:

And God declared that all of creation was indeed very good.

This scripture tells us that God loved creation – God created it, and gives us the opportunity to be in it, with it, sustaining it and caring for it as stewards. Genesis reminds us how many and varied are the gifts of creation we experience in life in this world.

On Earth Day, (and all the days to come) – in which we are most likely experiencing creation from our particular piece of the earth, let's look closely at the blade of grass, the trees, the flowers that are blooming and see the gift we've been given. Let's see the animals, the birds, the insects and notice how beautifully and wonderfully they are made. Let's decide to pay attention, give thanks and experience the blessing of the gifts we've been given.

Prayer:

Dear God, when earth day comes up on our calendars, it's an opportunity to take time to give thanks for the amazing creation you have given us. Help us to care for creation on a daily basis, to be attentive to what we are learning about living a simpler life. Help us to join you in loving creation and declaring it very good. In Jesus Name, Amen

Reflection Questions:

1) What do you notice because you paid attention to creation that you wouldn't have noticed otherwise?

2) What one thing can you do this week to care for creation?

3) What one lesson about living more simply do you want to make part of the way you live your life?

(18) A New Thing
Isaiah 43:18-19

> *Do not remember the former things or consider the things of old. I am about to do a new thing; now it springs forth, do you not perceive it? I will make a way in the wilderness and rivers in the desert.*

Devotion:

Even in the midst of the life we are living now – when many of us are thinking we just want to go back – these words feel right. We are on the verge of a new day – and just hoping to time travel back to what was – well that seems like we'd be missing the moment. What we've learned in this time matters. How we've listened, and noticed the world differently, how we've paid attention to what it means to love our neighbor, how we've figured out what is important to us – those are lessons we want to celebrate learning.

Today – there is the promise of resurrection – of new hope, of a new thing ready to be born. Let's not miss the moment. Let's open our eyes to see the new day that comes to us – and give thanks for the way in the wilderness, the rivers in the desert.

Prayer:

Dear God, help us O Lord to be present to the hope you plant in us. Help us to seek what will be with new eyes. Help us to love and serve you today – trusting that you will be with us in the time that is to come. In Jesus Name, Amen

Reflection Questions:

1) What have you learned lately that gives you hope for the future?

2) Where do you see possibilities in this day for hope and light to break through?

3) If you could paint a picture of the new thing you are hoping for right now – what would it look like?

(19) What is Love?
1 John 4:7-12

> *Beloved let us love one another, because love is from God; everyone who loves is born of God and knows God. Whoever does not love does not know God, for God is love. God's love was revealed among us in this way: God sent his only Son into the world so that we might live through him. In this is love, not that we loved God but that he loved us and sent his Son to be the atoning sacrifice for our sins. Beloved, since God loved us so much, we also ought to love one another. No one has ever seen God; if we love one another, God lives in us, and his love is perfected in us.*

Devotion:

What is Love? I mean – we kind of know, right? Or at least we feel like we do. We hear the word everywhere – in songs, in movies, in books - we love a love story.

But as people who follow Jesus – we also know there's more to it. We know that love has sacrifice in it. Christ gave his life for love of us. We know that loving people the way Christ loved us – is more than staying around while it feels good and moving on when it doesn't. We know that love asks us to challenge ourselves to practice compassion and empathy, to value other people at least as highly as we value ourselves. We learn that Jesus loves everybody and wants the same from us.

Right now – we might be feeling pushed to learn how to love in ways we've never had to figure out before. Being together all the time opens up whatever issues we've had and puts them right in front of us. So – it's a great time to practice love. To be patient, and kind, to be generous in spirit, to be slow to anger and quick to forgive. To rely on the love Christ has for us to be underneath our best attempts to show love to other people. Beloved – let us love one another. That is the wisdom of God's word, and it is the wisdom we really need to hear today.

Prayer:

Dear God, help me to practice love - to realize it is more than a feeling, and work my way through what love looks like now. How can I reflect your love today? Lord in your mercy, Hear my prayer. Amen

Reflection Questions:

1) What is love?

2) What have you learned about love in the last month?

3) What one aspect of love do you pray God shows through you this week?

(20) Filling Up
Psalm 42:1-2,4-5

As a deer longs for flowing streams, so my soul longs for you, O God.

My soul thirsts for God, for the living God.

When shall I come and behold the face of God? These things I remember, as I pour out my soul: how I went with the throng and led them in procession to the house of God, with glad shouts and songs of thanksgiving, a multitude keeping festival. Why are you cast down, O my soul, and why are you disquieted within me? Hope in God; for I shall again praise him, my help.

Devotion:

What are the memories that fill us up? What are the moments we can remember being with our faith community that give us strength? What reminds us of the story of times when our souls have been filled at the fountain of the Lord?

We are God's people – and God invites us to be filled up. One of the first camp songs I ever heard was based on this Psalm: As the Deer Panteth for the water – so my soul longeth after thee. You alone are my heart's desire, and I long to worship thee. You alone are my strength, my shield, to You alone may my spirit yield, You alone are my heart's desire and I long to worship thee. When I hear those words or sing them out loud or in my heart – I can feel their power bring me back to the day I first heard them, and I feel again the connection I felt to the Spirit of God in that moment in that place.

This is a time to let the stories of our personal faith journeys strengthen us for the current moment. To remember that no matter how alone we might feel on our journey – we are accompanied by the great company of the saints in the light, and we never walk alone.

Prayer:

Dear God, help us to remember times when we've felt filled up by your spirit. Show us your way and help us follow the light you shine into our lives. In Jesus Name, Amen

Reflection Questions:

1) What do you think the Psalmist means when he says his soul is thirsty?

2) Do you remember a time when you felt spiritually full?

3) What is one of the memories that lifts you up, when you need to be comforted by the Spirit of the Lord?

(21) Renewed Strength
Isaiah 40:28-31

> *Have you not known? Have you not heard? The LORD is the everlasting God, the Creator of the ends of the earth. He does not faint or grow weary; his understanding is unsearchable. He gives power to the faint and strengthens the powerless. Even youths will faint and be weary, and the young will fall exhausted.*
>
> *but those who wait for the LORD shall renew their strength, they shall mount up with wings like eagles, they shall run and not be weary, they shall walk and not faint.*

Devotion:

Those who wait for the Lord shall renew their strength.

I love that verse – especially in a moment of waiting. It's not about us getting ourselves in good enough shape to serve God again – it's about God renewing our strength, helping us be ready for the journey. We need to be reminded that we are not in this alone, especially now, when we are all behind walls, disconnected. I know that during the pandemic, I have needed to remind myself that it wasn't just happening to me – and the people I know – but that this is a whole world situation. We are not alone in getting tired of all the things that go along with this complicated time. Like loneliness, or overwhelm, or unemployment, or illness or grief – these are all real situations and real emotions. We need Isaiah to remind us that the Lord has the understanding we need, the power we need, and the Lord has the strength we need. Right now, is an opportunity to come to God in prayer, to ask God for help, to let ourselves rely on God's strength when we are feeling faint and weary.

May we hear and know that the Lord is the Everlasting God.

Prayer:

Dear God – I am needing your help remembering that you will renew my strength. Help me to wake each day refreshed and renewed in you. In Jesus Name, Amen

Reflection Questions:

1) What helps you when you feel overwhelmed or exhausted?

2) What would it take for God to recharge your batteries today?

3) What do you need most from God right now – strength, power, or understanding? Why did you pick that word?

(22) Beyond Boundaries
Numbers 11:24-30

> *So, Moses went out and told the people the words of the LORD; and he gathered seventy elders of the people and placed them all around the tent. Then the LORD came down in the cloud and spoke to him and took some of the spirit that was on him and put it on the seventy elders; and when the spirit rested upon them, they prophesied. But they did not do so again. Two men remained in the camp, one named Eldad, and the other named Medad, and the spirit rested on them; they were among those registered, but they had not gone out to the tent, and so they prophesied in the camp. And a young man ran and told Moses, "Eldad and Medad are prophesying in the camp." And Joshua son of Nun, the assistant of Moses, one of his chosen men, said, "My lord Moses, stop them!" But Moses said to him, "Are you jealous for my sake? Would that all the LORD's people were prophets, and that the LORD would put his spirit on them!" And Moses and the elders of Israel returned to the camp.*

Devotion:

One of those lessons in life that isn't easy to learn is that our sense that we are in control – is an illusion. Our best laid plans are not necessarily something we can count on. But that doesn't mean we despair. God is with us – and God's Holy Spirit is poured out – not just on us – but on all who are listening, paying attention and breathing it in.

In this passage, Moses has asked God for help, and God has spread the Holy Spirit on the people – and Moses is happy to hear that the Spirit is going even further than he thought it would. Some of his people are wanting more control – but Moses says in effect – "whoever isn't against us is for us." Jesus said that in Mark 9:40 when his disciples wanted other people to stop spreading good news without permission.

However, and wherever and in whomever we experience the Holy Spirit moving in these times, we need to be thankful, and pay attention – listen to what we're hearing – and trust that God is spreading God's vision far and wide.

Prayer:

Dear God, help me to trust that your Spirit is breaking in even now, to show us the way to follow you. Help me to look, to listen and to be faithful in how I respond. In Jesus Name, Amen

Reflection Questions:

1) Have you ever had an idea that felt like it came from more than your brain? Were you able to share it?

2) How does the idea that control is an illusion sit with you? Do you agree/disagree?

3) What helps you listen for God? Try slowing yourself down, and writing a prayer by hand, inviting God to be with you.

(23) Built Together
Ephesians 2:17-22

> *So Jesus came and proclaimed peace to you who were far off and peace to those who were near; for through him both of us have access in one Spirit to the Father. So then you are no longer strangers and aliens, but you are citizens with the saints and also members of the household of God, built upon the foundation of the apostles and prophets, with Christ Jesus himself as the cornerstone. In him the whole structure is joined together and grows into a holy temple in the Lord; in whom you also are built together spiritually into a dwelling place for God.*

Devotion:

This passage is one of my favorites for understanding the Trinity – the concept of three in one. Through Jesus we are built together in the image of the Creator God – and knitted together by the Holy Spirit that dwells in us, around us, between us.

Hope for today lives in those words.

Hope that underneath the surface, we are all made in the image of God.

Hope that the love of Christ can call us out of our separateness and toward being one body.

Hope that what is broken in us is being knit together with the love of the Spirit.

We are people of hope. We know that in Jesus we have learned that what looks like the end is not the end. We know that in the Spirit, we have a Comforter and an Advocate who will point us in the direction we need to go. We know that we were Created by a God who loves us – and wants us to love one another.

As we approach the Sunday known as Trinity Sunday in the Church Year – May we make room for the three in one to be in us and with us and show us the way.

Prayer:

Dear God, help us be and say and look forward to your love alive in this world – changing us in ways we can't imagine – but hope for every day. In Jesus Name, Amen

Reflection Questions:

1) What is the hope that helps you get through the days of your life?

2) How do the different parts of the Trinity make sense to you?

3) When you pray – do you see the Creator God, Jesus, the Holy Spirit?

(24) Lay Your Worries Down
Matthew 6:25,33-34

> *"Therefore, I tell you, do not worry about your life, what you will eat or what you will drink, or about your body, what you will wear. Is not life more than food, and the body more than clothing?*
>
> *But strive first for the kingdom of God and his righteousness, and all these things will be given to you as well.*
>
> *"So do not worry about tomorrow, for tomorrow will bring worries of its own. Today's trouble is enough for today.*

Devotion:

We live in an anxious world, in a very anxious time. We are worried about the pandemic of disease. We are worried that we, or people we love will get sick, and not get better. We are worried about another wave. We are worried that our jobs will disappear.

We are worried about the pandemic of racism. We are worried that as much as we want this to be a new day in our country in regard to the racism that has been under and above the surface since the very beginning – we are worried that we will let ourselves go back once again to the way things have always been. We are worried that we will miss the moment that has the potential to change everything. We are worried that we won't do what we can.

If all we do is worry – we are in real trouble. Now is the time to pay attention to God's kingdom trying to break in. Now is the time to learn, to grow, to speak – to decide to be better. Now is the time to pay attention to how we can care for other people. To notice the amazing gifts of God's creation that are for all of us and each of us – reminding us that we live in a world none of us created, and we enjoy gifts none of us earned. We were created to give and to share. God's kingdom asks us to put justice for all God's people ahead of our own agenda. Today – let us lay our worries down – and pick up the music of God's Kingdom breaking in.

Prayer:

Dear God, Open the eyes of our hearts Lord. Open the eyes of our hearts. Amen

Reflection Questions:

1) Right now, what part of the worry you are experiencing can you lay down?

2) What part of the Kingdom of God do you notice trying to break into your reality?

3) How is God opening the eyes of your heart today?

(25) Welcoming
Matthew 10:40-42

> *"Whoever welcomes you welcomes me, and whoever welcomes me welcomes the one who sent me. Whoever welcomes a prophet in the name of a prophet will receive a prophet's reward; and whoever welcomes a righteous person in the name of a righteous person will receive the reward of the righteous; and whoever gives even a cup of cold water to one of these little ones in the name of a disciple—truly I tell you, none of these will lose their reward."*

Devotion:

Welcoming – what does it look like today? Do we welcome people by including them in what we're doing? Do we welcome people by sharing what we can with them on-line? Do we welcome people by being safe – even when we'd rather be present?

It's a good time to consider welcoming. Reading these verses, it feels to me like welcoming has a lot to do with listening, respecting, hearing the other person. Welcoming feels like a way to acknowledge that God can work through us. Welcoming is about responding to the needs of the person in front of us – saying yes to what we can say yes to – sharing what we have to share. Welcoming includes remembering that in the Spirit we are together – connected no matter what.

Someone I know put a container of stew on people's doorsteps as a reminder of a good time of connection and love. It was a way to welcome them into celebrating what can still be celebrated together. She reminded the community that being the body of Christ together is about more than being in the same space.

So, what does welcome mean to you?

Prayer:

Dear God, please help me to remember the joy of welcoming and being welcomed, and work to be welcoming, no matter what the challenges. In Jesus Name, Amen

Reflection Questions:

1) Do you remember a time when you felt really welcome in a new place?

2) What specific things help you understand that you are welcome? What gets in the way of your being welcoming?

3) How can you reach out to someone to help them know that they are welcome?

(26) Discernment
Jeremiah 28:5-9

> *Then the prophet Jeremiah spoke to the prophet Hananiah in the presence of the priests and all the people who were standing in the house of the LORD; and the prophet Jeremiah said, "Amen! May the LORD do so; may the LORD fulfill the words that you have prophesied and bring back to this place from Babylon the vessels of the house of the LORD, and all the exiles. But listen now to this word that I speak in your hearing and in the hearing of all the people. The prophets who preceded you and me from ancient times prophesied war, famine, and pestilence against many countries and great kingdoms. As for the prophet who prophesies peace, when the word of that prophet comes true, then it will be known that the LORD has truly sent the prophet."*

Devotion:

When Jeremiah told the people to wait and see about who was really speaking the word of God, and who was just telling the people what they wanted to hear, he knew exactly what he was doing. He knew that the people would eventually understand that God wasn't about congratulating the people when they did what they wanted, and got what they wanted, especially at the expense of everyone else. Jeremiah had lived his life burning up with the word of God. He had been called to say things that were true, even when they were hard. The benefit of that experience was that Jeremiah could recognize the Word of God when he heard it from other people, and he could discern whether or not what he was hearing was just designed to make the speaker popular.

When we are listening for the Word of God, our role is to hear where God is pointing us, even when the direction isn't comfortable or easy. Sometimes, we need to ask ourselves if we have been creating God in our image. Does God always agree with our perspective? Maybe we haven't asked ourselves hard enough questions. Does God tell us what we want to hear? Maybe we haven't been listening for the things that will challenge us on our journey.

Prayer:

Dear God, help us to hear the words you have to say to us today. Help us to listen and decide to follow you – even if the direction looks challenging. Amen

Reflection Questions:

1) When have you found yourself trying to find the easy way out of a difficult decision?

2) What is the Word of God you are seeking today?

3) What is the question you need to ask God today?

(27) Meditating on our Faith
Psalm 145:1-5

I will extol you, my God and King, and bless your name forever and ever.

Every day I will bless you and praise your name forever and ever.

Great is the LORD, and greatly to be praised; his greatness is unsearchable.

One generation shall laud your works to another and shall declare your mighty acts. On the glorious splendor of your majesty, and on your wondrous works, I will meditate.

Devotion:

One generation shall share to the next.

That's the faith story many of us have. We learned what we know about God, we experienced our faith through the lens of our families' faith.

And then at some point – often during a long night of the soul – we begin to meditate on our faith – on the wonderous works of God – and we choose. We choose to embrace not just what we were taught to believe – but what we believe ourselves, from the inside out.

The story of Jesus life, death and resurrection – if we let it - it can change us. We can become people who care about people – who stand up for what we believe is right. We can become people who trust that the Spirit of God does not abandon us – even when things are not going the way we want them to at all.

May we join the Psalmist in trusting in God – and letting God's greatness provide the foundation we need to stand on in all times.

Prayer:

Dear God, help me to trust in you – to meditate on your steadfast presence no matter what is happening in the world. Help me to be open to letting you change me. Amen

Reflection Questions:

1) What are your faith stories?

2) What story of God's love do you want to meditate on today?

3) When have you experienced the life of Christ changing you?

(28) God's Word Breaking In
Isaiah 55:10-12

> *For as the rain and the snow come down from heaven, and do not return there until they have watered the earth, making it bring forth and sprout, giving seed to the sower and bread to the eater, so shall my word be that goes out from my mouth. It shall not return to me empty, but it shall accomplish that which I purpose, and succeed in the thing for which I sent it.*
>
> *For you shall go out in joy, and be led back in peace; the mountains and the hills before you shall burst into song, and all the trees of the field shall clap their hands.*

Devotion:

How do we hear God's word today? There are so many words spoken to us. Through 24-7 news coverage – through social media like Facebook and Instagram – so many words. How do we hear God's word today?

There's something in us that seeks truth – that wants to hear what's real. And nothing less will satisfy that desire. God comes to God's people in the middle of times of trouble – and in the middle of occasions of joy – and God lets us see that there is more to life than what we're hearing in the many, many words that surround us. The Bible speaks God's word to us – even now. God can speak through the words that were written on the page to a different people, and a different time. We know it's God's word, because it has not stopped speaking – and it has not stopped pointing us toward a time of peace, hope, and joy. Jesus, the living word, still shows us the way to new life. We aren't promised the way will be easy – but we do know that the way will be marked with a love of God and a love of neighbor that will change the way we see the world.

Prayer:

Dear God, help us to listen for your word today – to make room for all the ways you are breaking into life as we know it. In Jesus Name, Amen

Reflection Questions:

1) What Biblical story do you remember that helped you see the world through a different lens?

2) Is there a place, or a particular time that helps you be opened to listen for God's word?

3) This passage talks a lot about elements of nature. Do you have an outdoor story that feels like the sacred broke into the ordinary?

(29) An Undivided Heart
Psalm 86:11-13

> *Teach me your way, O LORD, that I may walk in your truth; give me an undivided heart to revere your name.*
>
> *I give thanks to you, O Lord my God, with my whole heart, and I will glorify your name forever. For great is your steadfast love toward me; you have delivered my soul from the depths of Sheol.*

Devotion:

What is dividing your heart today? I find it too easy in these times to find myself going in a lot of directions inside my head and heart. So many things want my attention. Many good things – which makes it that much harder to decide which direction to go in.

That's when it's especially important to stop. To breathe. To listen for the word of God that is planted in us to help us know how to be faithful in these times. Sometimes in order to say yes to God, we have to say no to something else.

The steadfast love of the Lord is always with us. And if we take the time to give thanks, to glorify God with our whole hearts – we will find the way to walk in God's truth – and be on the path that leads to peace.

Prayer:

Dear God, help me to open my heart to let you move in it. Help me to listen to you as you open your way – and lead me toward your steadfast love. Amen

Reflection Questions:

1) What is dividing your heart today?

2) How would your life change if God answered this prayer, and your heart was no longer divided?

3) What do you need to say no to today?

(30) Wisdom
1 Kings 3:5-12

> *At Gibeon the LORD appeared to Solomon in a dream by night; and God said, "Ask what I should give you." And Solomon said, "You have shown great and steadfast love to your servant my father David, because he walked before you in faithfulness, in righteousness, and in uprightness of heart toward you; and you have kept for him this great and steadfast love, and have given him a son to sit on his throne today. And now, O LORD my God, you have made your servant king in place of my father David, although I am only a little child; I do not know how to go out or come in. And your servant is in the midst of the people whom you have chosen, a great people, so numerous they cannot be numbered or counted. Give your servant therefore an understanding mind to govern your people, able to discern between good and evil; for who can govern this your great people?"*
>
> *It pleased the Lord that Solomon had asked this. God said to him, "Because you have asked this, and have not asked for yourself long life or riches, or for the life of your enemies, but have asked for yourself understanding to discern what is right, I now do according to your word. Indeed, I give you a wise and discerning mind; no one like you has been before you and no one like you shall arise after you.*

Devotion:

Solomon could have asked for anything in this moment – and what he asked for was discernment. He wanted to know what to do, how to be, how to lead – in a way that didn't just make him richer or stronger or more famous. He wanted to rule as a follower of God. He wanted to point toward the God he served. He wanted the decisions he made to be in line with what God wanted to see from him as a leader.

God tells Solomon, this is a good request. A good prayer. It was something God was happy to hear from him. If you've heard about Solomon – what you've likely heard is that he's most famous for his wisdom. His ability to stand in the middle of difficult situations and point toward genuine justice. To help people to do the right thing.

Right now, as we live in difficult times, more wisdom for ourselves, for our leaders, for all people – is a good prayer. To be wise in discernment, and gracious in our actions, walking in this world with eyes open, looking for places to see the chance to love with the love of God, and helping others to do the same – may this be our prayer.

Prayer:

Help me O Lord to have the wisdom to ask for wisdom for myself, and for all who lead – that we might find ways to connect our will with your way. Amen

Reflection Questions:

1) Where do you perceive wisdom in the world today?

2) How highly does wisdom place on your list of prayer requests?

3) Have you ever had a sense that a prayer for wisdom in your life has been answered?

(31) On the Heart
Jeremiah 31:31-34

> *The days are surely coming, says the LORD, when I will make a new covenant with the house of Israel and the house of Judah. It will not be like the covenant that I made with their ancestors when I took them by the hand to bring them out of the land of Egypt—a covenant that they broke, though I was their husband, says the LORD. But this is the covenant that I will make with the house of Israel after those days, says the LORD: I will put my law within them, and I will write it on their hearts; and I will be their God, and they shall be my people. No longer shall they teach one another, or say to each other, "Know the LORD," for they shall all know me, from the least of them to the greatest, says the LORD; for I will forgive their iniquity, and remember their sin no more.*

Devotion:

This passage – the new covenant passage – contains a gift that is worth holding unto – worth committing to memory. It tells us about a relationship with God that will be so strong, we will know it from the inside out. For the words will be written on our hearts.

This image is such a blessing. When we are vulnerable, when we feel abandoned, when we suffer – we are met in that place of pain by God's word. When we are full of love and joy, God's word is there for us. The new covenant – of deep forgiveness, and relationship without end - these words are for all God's people. Nothing we can do can separate us from that love.

"For the Lord says, I will be their God, and they shall be my people." This is the promise we stand on. This is the relationship that never ends.

Prayer:

Dear God, May I see and trust this day that your word is written on my heart. May I be open to the blessing of knowing you and being known by you. Amen

Reflection Questions:

1) Imagine God's word written on your heart – what do you see?

2) What are your experiences of coming to know God?

3) What does it mean to you to spend time with God?

(32) Sheer Silence
1 Kings 19:9-12

> *At that place he came to a cave and spent the night there. Then the word of the LORD came to him, saying, "What are you doing here, Elijah?" He answered, "I have been very zealous for the LORD, the God of hosts; for the Israelites have forsaken your covenant, thrown down your altars, and killed your prophets with the sword. I alone am left, and they are seeking my life, to take it away."*
>
> *He said, "Go out and stand on the mountain before the LORD, for the LORD is about to pass by." Now there was a great wind, so strong that it was splitting mountains and breaking rocks in pieces before the LORD, but the LORD was not in the wind; and after the wind an earthquake, but the LORD was not in the earthquake; and after the earthquake a fire, but the LORD was not in the fire; and after the fire a sound of sheer silence.*

Devotion:

How do you feel about this passage? Do you find it comforting to think that God comes to Elijah in the silence? Or do you wish God would be present in more obvious ways – visual – like a fire – or loud like an earthquake?

After all, Elijah's been through a lot on God's behalf. You'd think he'd want to be sure that what he's hearing now is God's voice, God's call to him. But – Elijah seems to be just fine hearing God show up in the silence. The sheer silence.

Have you ever experienced a moment that felt like sheer silence? Once I was in the Cathedral of Saint John the Divine for a concert. And the lights went down – and there was this moment – when 1000 people were silent – listening waiting together to hear what would come next. A voice came out of the balcony – way up above the floor – singing Silent Night. Beautiful, clear, angelic singing. I wonder how many of the 1000 people had the sense that God was breaking into that silence, pulling us out of our own pre-Christmas craziness and getting us to see that Christ breaks into our world.

It doesn't matter that it's not December. Christ is breaking into our world – and if we pay attention – and leave him space in our lives – we will hear him. In the silence, in the wind, in the rain – The Prince of Peace comes even now.

Prayer:

Dear God, we are in the midst of crazy times. We know that you know that. Help us to leave space for you to bring your word into our world. Amen

Reflection Questions:

1) Do you find it hard to be silent?

2) What helps you listen for God?

3) What do you think God wants you to pay attention to this week?

(33) Transformation
Romans 12:1-2

> *I appeal to you therefore, brothers and sisters, by the mercies of God, to present your bodies as a living sacrifice, holy and acceptable to God, which is your spiritual worship. Do not be conformed to this world, but be transformed by the renewing of your minds, so that you may discern what is the will of God— what is good and acceptable and perfect*

Devotion:

Transformation. What does that word mean to you? From talking to people over the years, I've heard a lot of different connotations that this word has for different people. Some think of the toys that were popular some years back – transformers. They were pretty cool – from a parent perspective, two toys for the price of one. Some think of corporate initiatives that went under the title Transformation Teams. One person told me a transformation specialist was the one that told her, her job had been transformed out of existence.

Today – I want to invite us to try to let this word be redefined in our lives. Let Paul's words in Romans encourage each of us to put aside conforming to this world and let transformation happen in us. Getting our wills aligned with a different vision for life in this world – that is the invitation of these verses. I wonder what kind of transformation work Jesus would lift up to each of us, if we prayed for this kind of help?

Here and now – there are lots of changes happening. We have lots of chances to let go of the way we've lived in the past and pick up the opportunity to live a transformed life!

Prayer:

Dear God, help me be open to your invitation to live a life that focusses on you – and your vision for how life in our world could be. May my will be aligned with yours! Amen

Reflection Questions:

1) Give yourself some time to think about the word transformation. What does it mean to you?

2) In what ways do you want to let go of conforming to this world?

3) How might you be an agent of transformation today?

(34) Moving Day
1 Corinthians 13:4-7, 12-13

Love is patient; love is kind; love is not envious or boastful or arrogant or rude. It does not insist on its own way; it is not irritable or resentful; it does not rejoice in wrongdoing but rejoices in the truth. It bears all things, believes all things, hopes all things, endures all things.

For now we see in a mirror, dimly, but then we will see face to face. Now I know only in part; then I will know fully, even as I have been fully known. And now faith, hope, and love abide, these three; and the greatest of these is love.

Devotion:

As I write this midweek meditation I am mid-way through the process of helping one of our children move to college. The purchases and the packing are complete; it is the delivery to campus that is the final step of the move.

It's a strange time we live in, but some things remain the same. Parenting includes pride and excitement, mixed with a bit of nerves, and a touch of grief at the ending of one chapter, as another begins. It is love in action - in all the words we hear the Apostle Paul say in this beautiful passage.

Human love is a glimpse into the mirror in which we see a reflection of the love of God in which we stand. It is a gift - an opportunity - a way to live out our faith. Faith, hope and love abide, these three. And the greatest of these is love.

Prayer:

Dear God, we thank you for the opportunities we have to embrace love in this life. Help us see and trust in your love, with us every step of the way. Amen

Reflection Questions:

1) What words would be on your list if you were asked to define love today?

2) Who needs to hear that you love them today?

3) How are you being challenged to practice loving patience today?

(35) Companions on the Journey
Jeremiah 15:16

> *Your words were found, and I ate them, and your words became to me a joy and the delight of my heart; for I am called by your name, O LORD, God of hosts.*

Devotion:

Jeremiah was the first prophet I really felt like I got to know. From the beginning verses where he says, "But I'm only a boy," and tries to get God to see that he's not old enough for this much responsibility – Jeremiah has always struck me as a very human vessel for God's word to dwell in. God reassures Jeremiah again and again that he will be with him on this mission for repentance, giving him words and images like the potter's wheel with its possibility of being made new. But Jeremiah still gets upset when people treat him badly for sharing the very challenging word he has to share – and he complains mightily to God. I remember the first time I read this book of the Bible – it felt shocking to me, how free Jeremiah feels to be really, really angry. But then – when the people are taken away into exile – Jeremiah does this really cool thing. He buys back some of the land, to very tangibly say – we will be back. This exile is for a moment – as we begin to understand better our relationship with God, and what it means for our lives.

"Your words were found, and I ate them." What an image. In Jeremiah – I feel as though I find a companion for the journey who knows what it is to be afraid and try to do the right thing anyway. He is a man who seems to have eaten God's word and let it become the nourishment for his life. Jeremiah doesn't promise an easy journey – and he doesn't let us get away with thinking following God's way won't make all that big of a difference. But, he does say God is forgiving, God is the potter who will continue to work with the clay. He does say God is steadfast and faithful in love for God's people, and ultimately, Jeremiah witnesses to the reality that ingesting the word of God does become a joy in us.

Prayer:

Dear God, Today, help me to keep my focus on you, to open myself to your word of repentance, and let it dwell in me as a way of life. Amen

Reflection Questions:

1) What verses of scripture do you feel like you've taken into your life?

2) How does reading and dwelling with scripture help you see the world around us right now?

3) Do you see any Biblical figures as companions for your journey?

(36) Proverbs for Today
Proverbs 4:20-23

My child be attentive to my words; incline your ear to my sayings. Do not let them escape from your sight; keep them within your heart.

For they are life to those who find them, and healing to all their flesh. Keep your heart with all vigilance, for from it flow the springs of life.

Devotion:

Proverbs was the favorite book of the Bible for a man from my congregation who lived to be 93. He always told me he needed the wisdom of God to make sense of the life he was living. Here, today we need help finding a way forward. We need healing. We need words that fill the broken places in our hearts.

So, what do we do? Lots of people I know are keeping their hearts these days by trying to put aside the voices that make them feel crazy, frustrated, hopeless. We need to pay attention to the state of our hearts – to choose to keep them full of wisdom, and peace, and justice, and love. All those things – they don't destroy our spirits – they can build us up into the people we want to be becoming, into the body of Christ working in the world.

Prayer:

Dear Lord, help me to plant your word of love in my heart this day. Help me to keep it with me, and let it fill me up all day long. Amen

Reflection Questions:

1) What words are you keeping close to you today? Try writing Romans 12:2, or Micah 6:8, or Luke 4:18 on a piece of paper to carry with you or place it next to you on your computer screen.

2) Have you tried setting notifications to let you know you've been too long on social media? Let's notice what is getting our attention today.

3) What wisdom have you gleaned lately that feels like it was a message from God?

(37) Seventy-seven times
Matthew 18:21-22

> *Then Peter came and said to him, "Lord, if another member of the church sins against me, how often should I forgive? As many as seven times?" Jesus said to him, "Not seven times, but I tell you, seventy-seven times.*

Devotion:

Forgiveness. Always at the top of any list of spiritual practices that we need to embrace to help us heal. Whether we are trying to find a way to forgive someone that we are fighting with or trying to find a way to forgive ourselves for falling short of our own standards – unforgiveness can feel like an open wound. Even when we begin to heal, we can get stuck replaying old conversations, revisiting the wound and re-injuring ourselves.

This passage - this interaction with Peter lets us know that Jesus knows just how hard this really is. Not seven times, but seventy-seven times. Not a little bit of countable forgiveness – but forgiveness that is part of our daily life. Forgiveness that helps us let go of our grievances and embrace the healing that comes from asking God to come into our brokenness and help us heal. Forgiveness that open us to our own need to be forgiven and be thankful that God is always looking for ways to help us accept and live in that grace.

Forgiveness. Where is it coming up in your journey today?

Prayer:

Dear God, please help me to open my eyes and my ears to my need to forgive and be forgiven. Help me lay down the need to be defensive so that my heart can truly heal. Amen

Reflection Questions:

1) When you hear this passage – is there a relationship that comes to mind? Imagine that person and count slowly to seventy-seven.

2) Is there a part of your own story that you have a hard time forgiving yourself for?

3) Jesus often challenges us to move into a place where we aren't comfortable. Can you think of another time in the scriptures that Jesus asks you to go somewhere you'd rather not go?

(38) Jonah, the Whale and Us
Jonah 1:1-4, 13-17, 2:10

Now the word of the LORD came to Jonah son of Amittai, saying, "Go at once to Nineveh, that great city, and cry out against it; for their wickedness has come up before me." But Jonah set out to flee to Tarshish from the presence of the LORD. He went down to Joppa and found a ship going to Tarshish; so, he paid his fare and went on board, to go with them to Tarshish, away from the presence of the LORD. But the LORD hurled a great wind upon the sea, and such a mighty storm came upon the sea that the ship threatened to break up.

Nevertheless the men rowed hard to bring the ship back to land, but they could not, for the sea grew more and more stormy against them. Then they cried out to the LORD, "Please, O LORD, we pray, do not let us perish on account of this man's life. Do not make us guilty of innocent blood; for you, O LORD, have done as it pleased you." So they picked Jonah up and threw him into the sea; and the sea ceased from its raging. Then the men feared the LORD even more, and they offered a sacrifice to the LORD and made vows. But the LORD provided a large fish to swallow up Jonah; and Jonah was in the belly of the fish three days and three nights. Then the LORD spoke to the fish, and it spewed Jonah out upon the dry land.

Devotion:

The story of Jonah is a story we might recognize from childhood – the whale (large fish) makes for interesting illustrations in a Children's Bible. The story of Jonah is also a story that is relatable to us, and our journeys here and now. We all have times in our lives when we sense that where we are supposed to go is not some place we desire to go. That what we are supposed to do, is not something we desire to do.

You and I, sometimes we run from things God wants from us and for us, and sometimes we end up in the belly of the whale. That's not factual – but it surely is true. We find ourselves lost, and confused and wanting to see what is next, with our vision obscured by our decision to run in the opposite direction of what we understand to be the will of God. And it takes turning toward God for us to find our lives again.

Prayer:

Dear God, help me to be listening to your directions, and be ready to answer your call. And when I don't, please help me find my way back to solid ground. Amen

Reflection Questions:

1) Can you remember a time that you ran in the opposite direction of what you felt like you were supposed to do?

2) What helped you find your way back from that moment?

3) Where are you in relation to the story of Jonah today?

(39) Pathways
Psalm 25:4-5

Make me to know your ways, O LORD; teach me your paths.

Lead me in your truth, and teach me, for you are the God of my salvation; for you I wait all day long.

Devotion:

Have you ever walked a labyrinth? A labyrinth is a spiritual tool that's been around for at least 1000 years. It looks like a maze, but it's not. There is only one path in, and that path will lead us into the center – though it will seem to take us in and out, closer and farther from the middle, until we find that we have found our way.

There are a lot of lessons to learn in this experience. We can quiet our mind and ask God to help us be centered on learning how to follow God's way. We can ask God's help with a specific issue. We can repeat scripture as we walk, letting it become part of the rhythm of our soul.

Once I walked a labyrinth, and I was looking ahead to see where the path was taking me, and I kind of lost my footing, and stepped out of the path I was supposed to be on. And it occurred to me that if I had been paying attention to where I was, I wouldn't have fallen off the path. How often is that true for us – that we miss the current moment, too busy wondering what's going to come next?

When we are honest with ourselves and with God – we know we need help finding our way. We need to learn. We need to let the wisdom of God show us what is true and teach us how-to walk-in God's ways.

Prayer:

Dear God, please help me to learn what you have to teach me today. Help me to value your wisdom and truth and make them the center of my life. Amen

Reflection Questions:

1) What are some lessons of faith you've learned in life so far?

2) How can you open yourself to learning from God at this point in your life?

3) What helps you imagine God with you as you go forward on the pathway of life?

(40) Unity
Psalm 133

How very good and pleasant it is when kindred live together in unity! It is like the precious oil on the head, running down upon the beard, on the beard of Aaron, running down over the collar of his robes.

It is like the dew of Hermon, which falls on the mountains of Zion. For there the LORD ordained his blessing, life forevermore.

Devotion:

Unity – it's a word that doesn't make a lot of examples come to mind in today's world. It might be nice to think unity is something that happens all the time – but in our passage the metaphors are not about everyday occurrences either. Unity is something to be valued – to be treasured. Unity is something we need to work for – even and especially when it seems really hard.

Oh – not unity as in we are all the same. That's not unity – that's playing pretend. We aren't all the same. We are brothers and sisters - children of God – that's where we can find our unity. That's where we find something to celebrate. We experience unity in the realization that God loves all of us. And we experience unity when we spread that love beyond ourselves.

So – what's the one step you can take today to work toward some version of unity? What wall of separation can you work on pulling down?

Prayer:

Dear God, help me be a person who values unity. Help me open my eyes to possibilities that I can't see right now. Amen

Reflection Questions:

1) Think about an example of unity in our world. What characteristics do you see?

2) Some words that I think of when I consider unity are peacemaking, respect, listening. What words come to mind for you?

3) What can you do today to try to bring a new version of unity into your life and God's world?

(41) Think on These Things
Philippians 4:8-9

Finally, beloved, whatever is true, whatever is honorable, whatever is just, whatever is pure, whatever is pleasing, whatever is commendable, if there is any excellence and if there is anything worthy of praise, think about these things. Keep on doing the things that you have learned and received and heard and seen in me, and the God of peace will be with you.

Devotion:

Think on these things. Do we do that?

Do we think on the things that are true and genuine, just and hopeful, the things that build us up?

Or do we dwell on the things that we aren't grateful for – the things that we are frustrated about – the things that drag us down?

This passage isn't meant to be a guilt trip, telling us another way in which we don't measure up. These words from Paul to the people of Philippi – they are said in love. They are meant to show us the path that is too easy for us to forget, the path that can lead us to a renewed joy in life.

It's so easy to let the bad news of life derail us. Today – let's look for what is worthy of praise and focus our hearts and minds on those things and see what a difference it makes in how we experience the day.

Prayer:

Dear God, I really want to be a person who is filled with the things that your word tells us to think on through these verses. Help me to do with you what I find hard to do on my own. Amen

Reflection Questions:

1) Think about your day yesterday. What thoughts filled you up?

2) What can you "think on" today that fits with Paul's words?

3) Write down one of the words in the verses that jumps out at you, and let it fill your thoughts today.

(42) Called by Name
Isaiah 45:1-3

> *Thus says the LORD to his anointed, to Cyrus, whose right hand I have grasped to subdue nations before him and strip kings of their robes, to open doors before him— and the gates shall not be closed:*
>
> *I will go before you and level the mountains, I will break in pieces the doors of bronze and cut through the bars of iron, I will give you the treasures of darkness and riches hidden in secret places, so that you may know that it is I, the LORD, the God of Israel, who call you by your name.*

Devotion:

In these verses – we meet the God who breaks into the world – and turns things upside down. Or really – upside right. This is the God who changes the way the world works so that we can recognize that God is God. That when God calls us by name – it isn't because we are God. It's because we are known by God.

There are days we wish for this God to break in. Maybe every day, we wish for this kind of obvious strength by which God makes things right. But on many days – God calls our name to make a small change in the world right around us. To point to God's power by the way we live out our faith in the goodness of God transforming the world we live in, day by day and night by night. To walk in justice and kindness, to lean into mercy – to live as people who believe that new life is possible.

Faith isn't easy. Faith is believing in the God we can't always see and living as people who have heard our name called.

Prayer:

Dear God, I am praying for change in our world today. I need to ask you to break in. If you want me to help, please open my ears to hear you calling my name. Amen

Reflection Questions:

1) As you go through this day, look for opportunities to live as one whose name has been called. What did you notice?

2) This is a passage that tells us that God is powerful. But we sometimes feel frustrated that God doesn't use God's power when we think God should. How can you imagine God breaking into the world today?

3) What is one barrier to justice, kindness, and mercy that God is calling your name to push against?

(43) What is in Our Hearts?
Deuteronomy 6:4-9

> *Hear, O Israel: The LORD is our God, the LORD alone. You shall love the LORD your God with all your heart, and with all your soul, and with all you might. Keep these words that I am commanding you today in your heart. Recite them to your children and talk about them when you are at home and when you are away, when you lie down and when you rise. Bind them as a sign on your hand, fix them as an emblem on your forehead, and write them on the doorposts of your house and on your gates.*

Devotion:

This passage invites us to understand just how it is that something can come to be in our hearts. What is in our hearts is what we recite - what we tell our children, our families. What is in our hearts is what we talk about when we're at home, and when we're away – which means what we talk about all the time.

What do we talk about? What do we tell our families about? What is getting our attention and becoming part of our hearts? Maybe even becoming Lord of our lives?

I don't think I'm alone when I say that I am giving too much of my time and attention to things I don't want in my heart. I want the love of God in my heart. I want the peace of Christ in my heart. I want the Holy Spirit breathing faith and hope and love through me, and I want to be grounded in my faith in the justice of God. What can I do today to put those things in my heart?

Prayer:

Dear God, help me to put my faith and trust in you. Help me to talk about you, to meditate on you, to stand on your love in these coming days. In Jesus Name, Amen

Reflection Questions:

1) What do you spend too much time thinking and talking about?

2) What do you think would help you remember that you are God's beloved child today?

3) Write the verse - "You shall love the Lord your God with all your heart, and with all your soul, and with all your strength" on a piece of paper and put it somewhere you can see it. Try reading it several times throughout the day.

(44) When I Am Afraid
Psalm 34:4-8

> *I sought the LORD, and he answered me, and delivered me from all my fears. Look to him, and be radiant; so, your faces shall never be ashamed.*
>
> *This poor soul cried, and was heard by the LORD, and was saved from every trouble.*
>
> *The angel of the LORD encamps around those who fear him and delivers them. O taste and see that the LORD is good; happy are those who take refuge in him.*

Devotion:

"The angel of the Lord encamps around those who fear him and delivers them."

Can we picture ourselves in this place – where the angel of the Lord surrounds us, protects us, defends us, delivers us? The word encamps makes me think about a place outdoors, maybe in front of a campfire, or walking next to a flowing stream – where my soul is not drowned out by the television or the to do list - where there is room for the angel of the Lord to find me, and comfort me when I am afraid.

We likely know from experience by now that God doesn't always answer our prayers in the way we'd like them answered. Sometimes the things we fear do come to pass. But in those times – we do not have to feel alone, and we do not have to feel defeated. Instead, we can taste and see that the Lord is still good. And we can picture ourselves in a place of refuge, strengthened for the journey ahead.

Prayer:

Dear God, help me to find a place in my heart, mind and body where I can be honest with you about what I fear. Help me to trust you with my fears and know that I do not hold them alone. Amen

Reflection Questions:

1) Where could you go, in person or in your imagination, to make space for the angel of the Lord to be with you?

2) Try writing your own Psalm, to give the things you fear to God.

3) What does it mean to you to taste and see that the Lord is good?

(45) Today!
Psalm 70:1,4-5

Be pleased, O God, to deliver me.

O LORD make haste to help me!

Let all who seek you rejoice and be glad in you. Let those who love your salvation say evermore, "God is great!" But I am poor and needy; hasten to me, O God!

You are my help and my deliverer; O LORD, do not delay!

Devotion:

We live in a specific place, a particular society, a moment in time. I don't know what our life together as people in community will look like as you read these words. But in any case – I imagine we will need help from the Lord. No one day will change the fact that we will need help to heal. And we will need help to walk together. We will need help that brings us to a new point as God's people.

Is what we need patience? Is it wisdom for the journey ahead? Is it breaking down walls that have put us against each other? Is it compassion for those who are afraid?

We need to cry out to the Lord – with all that we are. We need to ask God to help us through this journey and look for God to point us toward a road we can walk on to get to a place of peace and hope and love in this world.

Prayer:

Dear God, you know that we are all afraid of something. You know that we need you. Your hope and your love need to break in. In the words of the Psalmist – O Lord, do not delay! Amen

Reflection Questions:

1) What do you need from the Lord today?

2) Try writing down three things you believe you need from the Lord today – and leaving your words in plain sight, so you can pray them throughout the day.

3) What's one step forward you see today?

(46) Treasures
Matthew 6:19-21

> *"Do not store up for yourselves treasures on earth, where moth and rust consume and where thieves break in and steal; but store up for yourselves treasures in heaven, where neither moth nor rust consumes and where thieves do not break in and steal. For where your treasure is, there your heart will be also.*

Devotion:

What are the treasures of your life? When we are children, we imagine treasures as gold buried in cases - as they are in storybooks – found by luck and circumstance. When we become adults - the word treasure grows its meaning. Oh – it might still be the winnings from the lottery ticket that we imagine can change our lives. Or it might be the investments we made that will give us the future we are looking for. But in truth, our treasures go much deeper.

Treasures are the relationships that last beyond a moment – the ones that make memories that sustain us through our days. Treasures are the talents we put hard work into – that bring us joy for joy's own sake. Treasures are the parts of our character we rely on, like steadfastness and empathy, listening and genuineness.

In this passage from the Sermon on the Mount, we are invited to rely on the treasures that thieves cannot break in and steal. The ones that don't rust or rot with age and weather. Jesus wants us to invest ourselves in walking in the world as people of faith, people who love beyond the point when it's easy, and people who care about the people who have been pushed out of the way. Jesus invites us to follow him – and in that following, we will find our treasure.

Prayer:

Dear God, help me today to be open to the treasures of my life, and give them the time and attention they need to grow and thrive. Help me to see the treasures you have placed right in front of me. Amen

Reflection Questions:

1) What are the treasures of your life?

2) What do you need to let go of – in order to have more space for the treasures you want to grow?

3) How can you imagine following Jesus opening up your possibilities of finding treasure?

(47) Giving Thanks
Ephesians 1:15-19

> *I have heard of your faith in the Lord Jesus and your love toward all the saints, and for this reason I do not cease to give thanks for you as I remember you in my prayers. I pray that the God of our Lord Jesus Christ, the Father of glory, may give you a spirit of wisdom and revelation as you come to know him, so that, with the eyes of your heart enlightened, you may know what is the hope to which he has called you, what are the riches of his glorious inheritance among the saints, and what is the immeasurable greatness of his power for us who believe, according to the working of his great power.*

Devotion:

In this passage, the Apostle Paul gives thanks for one of the churches he has planted along the way of his journey proclaiming the love of Christ around the world. He's thankful for the love they have spread along the way. And he's praying for them that they might continue to know Christ in a way that lets the power of God's immeasurable gifts live in them.

It is a wonderful prayer – a beautiful hymn to the power of the Spirit of God that doesn't leave us where we are but moves in us to help us be more and more of who we were created to be. We aren't stuck. Maybe we feel like we are – but we aren't. I hear people describe today's life as though we are living scenes from the movie "Groundhog Day," repeating each day again and again. But you know what? The actual premise of that movie is that when given a chance to live the same day again and again, eventually the main character learns to live and love and move back into life in the world as a more loving, more fulfilled person.

We are invited to go deeper into our relationship with Jesus - and learn to hope with him. We are invited to let the power of the Spirit transform us so that we can stand in the peace and the power of God.

Prayer:

Dear God, we are looking for a new way to view the days in front of us. We need your help. Open our eyes to the potential for growth in this time. In Jesus Name, Amen

Reflection Questions:

1) What does it mean to you to get to know Jesus better? If you wanted to get to know a friend better, what would you do? How would you go about it?

2) How can you open the door to let today be different than yesterday on your faith journey?

3) What are you thankful for today?

(48) Happy Thanksgiving Eve!
Galatians 5:22-23

> *By contrast, the fruit of the Spirit is love, joy, peace, patience, kindness, generosity, faithfulness, gentleness, and self-control. There is no law against such things.*

Devotion:

I love that in this scripture, we hear that there is no law against love and peace, patience and kindness, generosity and faithfulness, gentleness and self-control. Thank goodness, because these are the places in life we feel most alive! At the intersection of these fruits of the spirit, we find fulfillment, we find grace, we find genuine and whole life.

Of course, we can't get good at those things by just trying really hard. There are too many temptations that get in the way. No, the journey to wholeness of life goes through the healing of the spirit that Christ calls us to embrace. And we find that through lifting up our hearts in prayer. We find that through loving God with all that we are. And – a challenge that many people today find really hard to accomplish – we find whole life through forgiveness and grace toward others and toward our own brokenness.

In this space and time, may we let ourselves give thanks for the accompaniment of the Lord Jesus, who knows what it is to be us. Jesus, who lived on earth, who knows how hard it is to be whole, and came to give us eternal love and life.

Prayer:

Dear God, you know me. You know my spirit and the places where I struggle. Help me this day to accept your help, and let your spirit come into the broken places that are holding me back from full life in you. In Jesus name, Amen

Reflection Questions:

1) What is getting in the way for you today? How are you feeling blocked from the fruits of the spirit?

2) Which fruit of the spirit is the hardest for you to imagine as part of your life? Do you believe the Spirit of God might be able to do in you that which you can't do for yourself?

3) What does it mean to you that Jesus understands what it is to be us? What particularly are you thankful Jesus understands?

(49) Overcoming Fear
Matthew 24:36-44

"But about that day and hour no one knows, neither the angels of heaven, nor the Son, but only the Father. For as the days of Noah were, so will be the coming of the Son of Man. For as in those days before the flood they were eating and drinking, marrying and giving in marriage, until the day Noah entered the ark, and they knew nothing until the flood came and swept them all away, so too will be the coming of the Son of Man. Then two will be in the field; one will be taken, and one will be left. Two women will be grinding meal together; one will be taken, and one will be left. Keep awake therefore, for you do not know on what day your Lord is coming. But understand this: if the owner of the house had known in what part of the night the thief was coming, he would have stayed awake and would not have let his house be broken into. Therefore you also must be ready, for the Son of Man is coming at an unexpected hour.

Devotion:

If we are being honest with ourselves, this passage sounds scary. But this time, when we're afraid, instead of telling us "Do not fear" in the way we usually hear in scripture, the words we hear are "Keep Awake!"

Keep awake to the presence of God – look for the signs of God breaking in. Once, a young teenage boy new to the concept of faith told me that he had been looking for God in his life, and in the middle of a really difficult athletic competition, he felt the light of the sunshine on him – and it felt all of a sudden like he wasn't alone in the race anymore. And he began to wonder – does God actually care about me?

Keep Awake - be attentive - the invitation in this scripture reading is to live our lives present to the presence!

Prayer:

Dear God open our eyes and our hearts to look for you. Keep us awake to see you active in our world. In Jesus Name, Amen

Reflection Questions:

1) What does active waiting mean to you?

2) How can you practice being alive in your life?

3) What does God want you to wake up to today?

(50) Accepting the Invitation to Repentance
Matthew 3:1-6

In those days John the Baptist appeared in the wilderness of Judea, proclaiming, "Repent, for the kingdom of heaven has come near." This is the one of whom the prophet Isaiah spoke when he said,

"The voice of one crying out in the wilderness:

'Prepare the way of the Lord, make his paths straight.'"

Now John wore clothing of camel's hair with a leather belt around his waist, and his food was locusts and wild honey. Then the people of Jerusalem and all Judea were going out to him, and all the region along the Jordan, and they were baptized by him in the river Jordan, confessing their sins.

Devotion:

My favorite definition of repentance comes from the Greek word metanoia. The English translation is "Turn around - all the way around. A complete change of heart." Repentance doesn't mean do a little better than yesterday. Sin a little less, steal a little less, lie a little less. Metanoia means turn all the way around. Walk another way – prepare a different road – do what you need to do to change directions.

We live in a complicated world – where struggles and joy exist side by side. Repentance invites us to choose to pay attention to Jesus, no matter where we are on the journey right now and follow him on the path he's leading us to walk.

Prayer:

Dear God, I want to follow Jesus. Keep my eyes open for opportunities to choose repentance – and turn all the way around to you. In Jesus Name, Amen

Reflection Questions:

1) How do you define repentance?

2) Spend some time honestly praying to God to hear where repentance is calling your name today.

3) What do you need to clear out of the road to prepare to repent?

(51) The Wolf and the Lamb
Isaiah 11:1-2, 6-7

A shoot shall come out from the stump of Jesse, and a branch shall grow out of his roots. The spirit of the LORD shall rest on him, the spirit of wisdom and understanding, the spirit of counsel and might, the spirit of knowledge and the fear of the LORD.

The wolf shall live with the lamb, the leopard shall lie down with the kid, the calf and the lion and the fatling together, and a little child shall lead them. The cow and the bear shall graze; their young shall lie down together; and the lion shall eat straw like the ox.

Devotion:

These verses feel like the words we need to hear in order to find the healing power of forgiveness. To believe in the lying down of the wolf and the lamb is to believe that forgiveness and peace are possible.

We can begin by opening ourselves up to imagining the wolf and the lamb at peace together. How can this image help us embrace the power of God's forgiveness that lives for us, in us, through us?

As we look at this powerful image in our mind's eye - how do we imagine it coming to life today? In our personal lives, in our society, in our world?

Prayer:

Dear God - Help me to see where I need to open myself to forgiveness and the possibility of peace today. Especially help me to experience your forgiveness for me - and begin to understand the peace that is possible in you. In Jesus Name, Amen

Reflection Questions:

1) What's the hardest part of imagining peace in the world for you?

2) Can you imagine a scene like the one in the scripture reading in our world? Where are you in the scene?

3) Ask God's help with whatever feels unforgiven and not at peace in you today.

(52) Merry Christmas!
John 1:1-4, 14

In the beginning was the Word, and the Word was with God, and the Word was God. He was in the beginning with God. All things came into being through him, and without him not one thing came into being. What has come into being in him was life, and the life was the light of all people.

And the Word became flesh and lived among us, and we have seen his glory, the glory as of a father's only son, full of grace and truth.

Devotion:

And the Word Became Flesh!

Do you hear it?

Really hear it?

God cares enough about us, and the life we live in this world to become flesh, to live in it with us. The Word is God, in the beginning. Just like in Genesis, we hear the news that God is with us in this world from the beginning. Through the baby Jesus, God breaks in and shows us what our lives are really all about – how we are supposed to be in this together, how the last shall be first and the oppressed shall go free. Jesus turns it all upside down! Following Jesus turns our lives upside down too!

Through Jesus, we open our eyes to grace and truth. May the light of Christ shine in us!

Merry Christmas!

Prayer:

Dear God, I am grateful that you came to this world, became flesh and showed us so clearly that you know what it is to be us. Thank You! Amen

Reflection Questions:

1) How can you keep the birth of Christ in your vision as you celebrate Christmas this year?

2) Do you see Jesus breaking into the world this December?

3) Take some time to read one of the versions of the Christmas story, and give thanks for the Word becoming flesh!

www.ingramcontent.com/pod-product-compliance
Lightning Source LLC
Chambersburg PA
CBHW052108110526
44592CB00013B/1522